THE ORDER *of* CELEBRATING Matrimony

within Mass

redemptorist
publications

The Order of Celebrating Matrimony within Mass

Published by **Redemptorist Publications**
Alphonsus House, Chawton, Hampshire, GU34 3HQ
Email rp@rpbooks.co.uk, www.rpbooks.co.uk
A registered charity limited by guarantee.
Registered in England 3261721.

First published 1975
This revised edition first published January 2016

General Editor: Denis McBride C.Ss.R.
Editor: Peter Edwards
Design: Eliana Thompson

ISBN 978-0-85231-450-0

The *Order for Celebrating Matrimony* was granted *recognitio* by the
Congregation for Divine Worship and the Discipline of the Sacraments
for the dioceses of the Bishops' Conference of England and Wales on
19 March 2015, Prot. No. 88/15/L.

Concordat cum originali Jane Porter
Imprimatur + Peter Doyle, Bishop of Northampton
24 November 2015
Permission granted for distribution in diocese of Scotland.

Printed by Portland Print, Kettering, NN16 8UN

Contents

The Order of Celebrating Matrimony within Mass

The Introductory Rites

All stand for the entrance procession. The celebrant greets the bride and groom and leads them to the seats prepared for them. A hymn may be sung (see pp. 54-63) or the following Entrance Antiphon may be said or sung:

**May the Lord send you help from the holy place,
and give you support from Sion.
May he grant you your hearts' desire
and fulfil every one of your designs (alleluia).**

Greeting the People

All make the Sign of the Cross:

Priest: In the name of the Father, and of the Son, and of the Holy Spirit.

People: **Amen.**

The priest greets the people in one of these ways:

The grace of our Lord Jesus Christ,
and the love of God,
and the communion of the Holy Spirit
be with you all.

or

Grace to you and peace from God our Father
and the Lord Jesus Christ.

or

The Lord be with you.
And with your spirit.

We have come rejoicing into the house of the Lord
for this celebration, dear brothers and sisters,
and now we stand with N. and N.
on the day they intend to form a home of their own.
For them this is a moment of unique importance.
So let us support them
with our affection,
with our friendship,
and with our prayer as their brothers and sisters.
Let us listen attentively with them
to the word that God speaks to us today.
Then, with holy Church,
let us humbly pray to God the Father,
through Christ our Lord,
for this couple, his servants,
that he lovingly accept them,
bless them,
and make them always one.

or

N. and N., the Church shares your joy
and warmly welcomes you,
together with your families and friends,
as today,
in the presence of God our Father,
you establish between yourselves
a lifelong partnership.
May the Lord hear you on this your joyful day.
May he send you help from heaven and protect you.
May he grant you your hearts' desire
and fulfil every one of your prayers.

The Penitential Act is omitted.

The Gloria

The Gloria is said or sung:

**Glory to God in the highest,
and on earth peace to people of good will.**

**We praise you,
we bless you,
we adore you,
we glorify you,
we give you thanks for your great glory,
Lord God, heavenly King,
O God, almighty Father.**

**Lord Jesus Christ, Only Begotten Son,
Lord God, Lamb of God, Son of the Father,
you take away the sins of the world,
    have mercy on us;
you take away the sins of the world,
    receive our prayer;
you are seated at the right hand of the Father,
    have mercy on us.**

**For you alone are the Holy One,
you alone are the Lord,
you alone are the Most High,
Jesus Christ,
with the Holy Spirit,
in the glory of God the Father.
Amen.**

The Collect

Let us pray.

Pray silently for the bride and bridegroom; then either:

Be attentive to our prayers, O Lord,
and in your kindness uphold
what you have established
   for the increase of the human race,
so that the union you have created
may be kept safe by your assistance.
Through our Lord Jesus Christ, your Son,
who lives and reigns with you
   in the unity of the Holy Spirit,
one God, for ever and ever.
Amen.

or

O God, who in creating the human race
willed that man and wife should be one,
join, we pray, in a bond of inseparable love
these your servants who are to be united
   in the covenant of Marriage,
so that, as you make their love fruitful,
they may become, by your grace,
   witnesses to charity itself.
Through our Lord Jesus Christ, your Son,
who lives and reigns with you
   in the unity of the Holy Spirit,
one God, for ever and ever.
Amen.

A further selection of prayers will be found on pp. 28-29.

The Liturgy of the Word

All sit.
During the Liturgy of the Word there may be brief periods of silence for prayerful reflection.

First Reading

At the end of the reading, the reader acclaims:

The word of the Lord.
Thanks be to God.

Psalm

The cantor or reader sings or says the Psalm, and all make the response.

Second Reading

There may be another reading before the Gospel, at the end of which the reader acclaims:

The word of the Lord.
Thanks be to God.

Gospel

All stand.
The Alleluia or Acclamation may be sung or said to welcome the Gospel. The deacon or priest says:

The Lord be with you.
And with your spirit.

A reading from the holy Gospel according to N.
Glory to you, O Lord.

At the end of the Gospel, the deacon or priest acclaims:
The Gospel of the Lord.
Praise to you, Lord Jesus Christ.

The Homily

All sit.
The homily is now preached. At the end there may be a brief period of silence for reflection.

The Celebration of Marriage

All stand, including the bride and bridegroom, and the priest addresses them in these or similar words:

Dearly beloved,
you have come together into the house of the Church,
so that in the presence of the Church's minister
   and the community
your intention to enter into Marriage
may be strengthened by the Lord with a sacred seal.
Christ abundantly blesses the love that binds you.
Through a special Sacrament,
he enriches and strengthens
those he has already consecrated by Holy Baptism,
that they may be faithful to each other for ever
and assume all the responsibilities of married life.
And so, in the presence of the Church,
I ask you to state your intentions.

The Questions before the Consent

The following question is asked once only, but the bride and bridegroom answer separately.

N. and N., have you come here to enter into Marriage without coercion,
freely and wholeheartedly?

Bridegroom: **I have.**
Bride: **I have.**

N., are you resolved to take N. to be your wife:
to love her, comfort her, honour and protect her,
and forsaking all others, to be faithful to her
as long as you both shall live?

Bridegroom: **I am.**

N., are you resolved to take N. to be your husband:
to love him, comfort him, honour and protect him,
and forsaking all others, to be faithful to him
as long as you both shall live?

Bride: **I am.**

The following question may be omitted if, for example, the
couple is advanced in years.

Are you prepared to accept children lovingly from God
and to bring them up
according to the law of Christ and his Church?

Bridegroom: **I am.**
Bride: **I am.**

The Civil Declaration of Freedom

The law of England and Wales requires the couple to make a declaration of their freedom to marry, in one of the following forms, A, B or C. Names and surnames must be used.

A

The priest asks the bridegroom:
Are you, A.B., free lawfully to marry C.D.?

Bridegroom: **I am.**

The priest asks the bride:
Are you, C.D., free lawfully to marry A.B.?

Bride: **I am.**

or

B

The bridegroom reads the following or repeats the words after the priest:
**I do solemnly declare
that I know not of any lawful impediment
   why I, A.B.,
may not be joined in matrimony to C.D.**

The bride reads the following or repeats the words after the priest:
**I do solemnly declare
that I know not of any lawful impediment
   why I, C.D.,
may not be joined in matrimony to A.B.**

or

C

Bridegroom:

**I declare that I know of no legal reason
why I, A.B.,
may not be joined in marriage to C.D.**

Bride:

**I declare that I know of no legal reason
why I, C.D.,
may not be joined in marriage to A.B.**

The Consent

The priest invites the couple to declare their consent:

Since it is your intention
to enter the covenant of Holy Matrimony,
join your right hands and declare your consent
before God and his Church.

They join their right hands.

The couple face each other. The bridegroom and bride read
one of the following forms, A or B, or repeat the words after
the priest. Names and surnames must be used.

A

Bridegroom:

**I call upon these persons here present to witness
that I, A.B., do take thee, C.D.,
to be my lawful wedded wife,
to have and to hold from this day forward
for better, for worse,
for richer, for poorer,
in sickness and in health,
to love and to cherish
till death do us part.**

Bride:

**I call upon these persons here present to witness
that I, C.D., do take thee, A.B.,
to be my lawful wedded husband,
to have and to hold from this day forward,
for better, for worse,
for richer, for poorer,
in sickness and in health,
to love and to cherish
till death do us part.**

or

B

Bridegroom:

**I, A.B., take you (thee), C.D., to be my wedded wife
to have and to hold from this day forward,
for better, for worse,
for richer, for poorer,
in sickness and in health,
to love and to cherish
till death do us part.**

Bride:

**I, C.D., take you (thee), A.B.,
   to be my wedded husband
to have and to hold from this day forward,
for better, for worse,
for richer, for poorer,
in sickness and in health,
to love and to cherish
till death do us part.**

The Reception of the Consent

Receiving their consent, the priest says to the bride and bridegroom:

May the Lord in his kindness strengthen the consent
you have declared before the Church,
and graciously bring to fulfilment
   his blessing within you.
What God joins together, let no one put asunder.

or

May the God of Abraham, the God of Isaac,
   the God of Jacob,
the God who joined together our
   first parents in paradise,
strengthen and bless in Christ
the consent you have declared before the Church,
so that what God joins together,
   let no one may put asunder.

The priest invites those present to praise God:

Let us bless the Lord.
Thanks be to God.

Another acclamation may be sung or said.

The Blessing and Giving of Rings

The priest now blesses the ring(s).
One of the following forms may be used:

May the Lord bless ✠ these rings,
which you will give to each other
as a sign of love and fidelity.
Amen.

or

Bless, O Lord, these rings,
which we bless ✠ in your name,
so that those who wear them
may remain entirely faithful to each other,
abide in peace and in your will,
and live always in mutual charity.
Through Christ our Lord.
Amen.

or

Bless ✠ and sanctify your servants
in their love, O Lord,
and let these rings, a sign of their faithfulness,
remind them of their love for one another.
Through Christ our Lord.
Amen.

Using one of the following forms, the husband places his
wife's ring on her ring finger, saying:
**N., I give you this ring as a sign of our marriage:
with my body I honour you,
all that I am I give to you,
and all that I have I share with you,
in the name of the Father, and of the Son,
    and of the Holy Spirit.**
All: **Amen.**

The wife places her husband's ring on his ring finger, saying:

**N., I give you this ring as a sign of our marriage:
with my body I honour you,
all that I am I give to you,
and all that I have I share with you,
in the name of the Father, and of the Son,
    and of the Holy Spirit.**
All: **Amen.**

or

The husband places his wife's ring on her ring finger, saying:

**N., receive this ring
as a sign of my love and fidelity.
In the name of the Father, and of the Son,
and of the Holy Spirit.**

The wife places her husband's ring on his ring finger, saying:

**N., receive this ring
as a sign of my love and fidelity.
In the name of the Father, and of the Son,
and of the Holy Spirit.**

A hymn may be sung (see pp. 54-63).

The Prayer of the Faithful
(Bidding Prayers)

After each intention there is a pause while all pray. This time of silent prayer may be followed by the next intention, or by a response such as:

Lord, we ask you, hear our prayer.

A selection of bidding prayers can be found on pp. 52-53.

The Profession of Faith

On Sundays and Solemnities the Profession of Faith follows (see pp. 50-51).

The Liturgy of the Eucharist

All sit.
A hymn may be sung (see pp. 54-63), and the bread and wine for the celebration are brought to the altar. The priest offers prayers of blessing. If these are said aloud, all make the acclamation at the end of each prayer:

Blessed are you, Lord God of all creation,
for through your goodness we have received
the bread we offer you:
fruit of the earth and work of human hands,
it will become for us the bread of life.
Blessed be God for ever.

Blessed are you, Lord God of all creation,
for through your goodness we have received
the wine we offer you:
fruit of the vine and work of human hands,
it will become our spiritual drink.
Blessed be God for ever.

All stand when the priest says:
Pray, brethren (brothers and sisters),
that my sacrifice and yours
may be acceptable to God,
the almighty Father.

May the Lord accept the sacrifice at your hands
for the praise and glory of his name,
for our good
and the good of all his holy Church.

The priest says the Prayer over the Offerings, of which the following is one form. Alternatives are available on p. 29.

Receive, we pray, O Lord,
the offering made on the occasion
of this sealing of the sacred bond of Marriage,
and, just as your goodness is its origin,
may your providence guide its course.
Through Christ our Lord.
Amen.

The Eucharistic Prayer

The Lord be with you.
And with your spirit.

Lift up your hearts.
We lift them up to the Lord.

Let us give thanks to the Lord our God.
It is right and just.

The priest continues, giving praise and thanks to God. (See Prefaces on pp. 31-33.) Then all join together to sing or say:

Holy, Holy, Holy Lord God of hosts.
Heaven and earth are full of your glory.
Hosanna in the highest.
Blessed is he who comes in the name of the Lord.
Hosanna in the highest.

Then the people kneel, and the priest continues with the Eucharistic Prayer. Texts for the Eucharistic Prayers can be found on pp. 34-46.

After the words of consecration, the priest says:
The mystery of faith.

The people sing or say:

**We proclaim your Death, O Lord,
and profess your Resurrection
until you come again.**

or

**When we eat this Bread and drink this Cup,
we proclaim your Death, O Lord,
until you come again.**

or

**Save us, Saviour of the world,
for by your Cross and Resurrection
you have set us free.**

At the conclusion of the Eucharistic Prayer the priest takes the chalice and the paten with the host and, raising both, he sings or says:

Through him, and with him, and in him,
O God, almighty Father,
in the unity of the Holy Spirit,
all glory and honour is yours,
for ever and ever.
Amen.

The Communion Rite
The Lord's Prayer

All stand.

At the Saviour's command
and formed by divine teaching,
we dare to say:
**Our Father, who art in heaven,
hallowed be thy name;
thy kingdom come,
thy will be done
on earth as it is in heaven.
Give us this day our daily bread,
and forgive us our trespasses,
as we forgive those who trespass against us;
and lead us not into temptation,
but deliver us from evil.**

The Nuptial Blessing

The priest, facing the bride and bridegroom, gives the
Nuptial Blessing, of which the following is one form.
Alternatives can be found on pp. 47-49.

In the invitation, the words in parentheses are omitted if
either or both of the couple will not be receiving Holy
Communion.
In the prayer, the words in parentheses may be omitted
if circumstances suggest it, for example, if the bride and
bridegroom are advanced in years.

Dear brothers and sisters,
let us humbly pray to the Lord
that on these his servants, now married in Christ,
he may mercifully pour out
the blessing of his grace
and make of one heart in love
(by the Sacrament of Christ's Body and Blood)
those he has joined by a holy covenant.

All pray silently for a short while.

O God, who by your mighty power
created all things out of nothing,
and, when you had set in place
the beginnings of the universe,
formed man and woman in your own image,
making the woman an inseparable helpmate to the man,
that they might no longer be two, but one flesh,
and taught that what you were pleased to make one
must never be divided;

O God, who consecrated the bond of Marriage
by so great a mystery
that in the wedding covenant you foreshadowed
the Sacrament of Christ and his Church;

O God, by whom woman is joined to man
and the companionship they had in the beginning
is endowed with the one blessing
not forfeited by original sin
nor washed away by the flood.

Look now with favour on these your servants,
joined together in Marriage,
who ask to be strengthened by your blessing.
Send down on them the grace of the Holy Spirit
and pour your love into their hearts,
that they may remain faithful in the Marriage covenant.

May the grace of love and peace
abide in your daughter N.,
and let her always follow the example of those holy women
whose praises are sung in the Scriptures.
May her husband entrust his heart to her,
so that, acknowledging her as his equal
and his joint heir to the life of grace,
he may show her due honour
and cherish her always

with the love that Christ has for his Church.

And now, Lord, we implore you:
may these your servants
hold fast to the faith and keep your commandments;
made one in the flesh,
may they be blameless in all they do;
and with the strength that comes from the Gospel,
may they bear true witness to Christ before all;
(may they be blessed with children,
and prove themselves virtuous parents,
who live to see their children's children).

And grant that,
reaching at last together the fullness of years
for which they hope,
they may come to the life of the blessed
in the Kingdom of Heaven.
Through Christ our Lord.
Amen.

The Peace

The peace of the Lord be with you always.
And with your spirit.

Let us offer each other the sign of peace.

The bride and bridegroom and all present offer one another
the customary sign of peace, which is an expression of peace,
communion and charity.

The Breaking of the Bread

The following is said or sung as the priest takes the host, breaks it and places a small piece in the chalice.

Lamb of God, you take away the sins of the world, have mercy on us.
Lamb of God, you take away the sins of the world, have mercy on us.
Lamb of God, you take away the sins of the world, grant us peace.

Invitation to Communion

The people kneel.
The priest raises the host and says:

Behold the Lamb of God,
behold him who takes away the sins of the world.
Blessed are those called to the supper of the Lamb.
Lord, I am not worthy
that you should enter under my roof,
but only say the word
and my soul shall be healed.

After the priest has consumed the Body and Blood of Christ, the communicants come forward in reverent procession to receive Communion. A hymn may be sung (see pp. 54-63), or a Communion Antiphon such as the following may be said or sung:

Christ loved the Church and handed himself over for her,
to present her as a holy and spotless bride for himself (alleluia).

The priest or minister shows the host to each of the communicants, saying:

The Body of Christ.
Amen.

When Communion is ministered under both kinds, the minister of the chalice raises it slightly and shows it to each of the communicants, saying:

The Blood of Christ.
Amen.

After the distribution of Communion, if appropriate, a silence may be observed for a while, or a hymn may be sung (see pp. 54-63).

Prayer after Communion

The priest says, or sings, the Prayer after Communion, of which the following is one form:

Let us pray.
Pause for silent prayer

By the power of this sacrifice, O Lord,
accompany with your loving favour
what in your providence you have instituted,
so as to make of one heart in love
those you have already joined in this holy union
(and replenished with the one Bread
    and the one Chalice).
Through Christ our Lord.
Amen.

Alternative prayers will be found on p. 30.

The Concluding Rites
Solemn Blessing at the End of Mass

The Lord be with you.
And with your spirit.

Bow down for the blessing.

Before blessing the people, the priest blesses the bride and bridegroom, in a form such as the following:

May God the eternal Father
keep you of one heart in love for one another,
that the peace of Christ may dwell in you
and abide always in your home.
Amen.

May you be blessed in your children,
have solace in your friends
and enjoy true peace with everyone.
Amen.

May you be witnesses in the world to God's charity,
so that the afflicted and needy
    who have known your kindness
may one day receive you thankfully
into the eternal dwelling of God.
Amen.

He then blesses all present:

And may almighty God bless all of you,
    who are gathered here,
the Father, and the Son, ✠ and the Holy Spirit.
Amen.

The Dismissal

Then the deacon or the priest says:

Go forth, the Mass is ended.

or

Go and announce the Gospel of the Lord.

or

Go in peace, glorifying the Lord by your life.

or

Go in peace.
Thanks be to God.

The Civil Register

The newly married couple, together with the witnesses, go to sign the civil register.

A hymn may be sung (see pp. 54-63).

Appendix A
Collects

Be attentive to our prayers, O Lord,
and in your kindness
pour out your grace on these your servants
   (N. and N.),
that, coming together before your altar,
they may be confirmed in love for one another.
Through our Lord Jesus Christ, your Son,
who lives and reigns with you
   in the unity of the Holy Spirit,
one God, for ever and ever.
Amen.

O God, who consecrated the bond of Marriage
by so great a mystery
that in the wedding covenant you foreshadow
the Sacrament of Christ and his Church,
grant, we pray, to these your servants,
that what they receive in faith
they may live out in deeds.
Through our Lord Jesus Christ, your Son,
who lives and reigns with you
   in the unity of the Holy Spirit,
one God, for ever and ever.
Amen.

Grant, we pray, almighty God,
that these your servants,
now to be joined by the Sacrament of Matrimony,
may grow in the faith they profess
and enrich your Church with faithful offspring.
Through our Lord Jesus Christ, your Son,
who lives and reigns with you
   in the unity of the Holy Spirit,
one God, for ever and ever.
Amen.

O God, who since the beginning of the world
have blessed the increase of offspring,
show favour to our supplications
and pour forth the help of your blessing
on these your servants (N. and N.),
so that in the union of Marriage
they may be bound together
in mutual affection,
in likeness of mind,
and in shared holiness.
Through our Lord Jesus Christ, your Son,
who lives and reigns with you
    in the unity of the Holy Spirit,
one God, for ever and ever.
Amen.

Prayers over the Offerings

Receive in your kindness, Lord,
the offerings we bring in gladness before you,
and in your fatherly love
watch over those you have joined
    in a sacramental covenant.
Through Christ our Lord.
Amen.

Show favour to our supplications, O Lord,
and receive with a kindly countenance
the oblations we offer for these your servants,
joined now in a holy covenant,
that through these mysteries
they may be strengthened
in love for one another and for you.
Through Christ our Lord.
Amen.

Prayers after Communion

Having been made partakers at your table,
we pray, O Lord,
that those who are united by the Sacrament of Marriage
may always hold fast to you
and proclaim your name to the world.
Through Christ our Lord.
Amen.

Grant, we pray, almighty God,
that the power of the Sacrament we have received
may find growth in these your servants
and that the effects of the sacrifice we have offered
may be felt by us all.
Through Christ our Lord.
Amen.

Appendix B

Prefaces

A

The dignity of the Marriage covenant.

It is truly right and just, our duty and our salvation,
always and everywhere to give you thanks,
Lord, holy Father, almighty and eternal God.

For you have forged the covenant of marriage
as a sweet yoke of harmony
and an unbreakable bond of peace,
so that the chaste and fruitful love of holy Matrimony
may serve to increase the children you adopt as your own.

By your providence and grace, O Lord,
you accomplish the wonder of this twofold design:
that, while the birth of children brings
    beauty to the world,
their rebirth in Baptism gives increase to the Church,
through Christ our Lord.

Through him, with the Angels and all the Saints,
we sing the hymn of your praise,
as without end we acclaim:
Holy, Holy, Holy Lord God of hosts…

B

The great Sacrament of Matrimony.

It is truly right and just, our duty and our salvation,
always and everywhere to give you thanks,
Lord, holy Father, almighty and eternal God,
through Christ our Lord.

For in him you have made a new covenant
    with your people,
so that, as you have redeemed man and woman
by the mystery of Christ's Death and Resurrection,
so in Christ you might make them
    partakers of divine nature
and joint heirs with him of heavenly glory.

In the union of husband and wife
you give a sign of Christ's loving gift of grace,
so that the Sacrament we celebrate
might draw us back more deeply
into the wondrous design of your love.

And so, with the Angels and all the Saints,
we praise you, and without end we acclaim:
Holy, Holy, Holy Lord God of hosts...

C

Matrimony as a sign of divine love.

It is truly right and just, our duty and our salvation,
always and everywhere to give you thanks,
Lord, holy Father, almighty and eternal God.

For you willed that the human race,
created by the gift of your goodness,
should be raised to such high dignity
that in the union of husband and wife
you might bestow a true image of your love.

For those you created out of charity
you call to the law of charity without ceasing
and grant them a share in your eternal charity.

And so, the Sacrament of holy Matrimony,
as the abiding sign of your own love,
consecrates the love of man and woman,
through Christ our Lord.

Through him, with the Angels and all the Saints,
we sing the hymn of your praise,
as without end we acclaim:
Holy, Holy, Holy Lord God of hosts...

Appendix C
Eucharistic Prayers

Eucharistic Prayer I
(The Roman Canon)

The words in parentheses may be omitted.

Priest: To you, therefore, most merciful Father,
we make humble prayer and petition
through Jesus Christ, your Son, our Lord:
that you accept
and bless ✠ these gifts, these offerings,
these holy and unblemished sacrifices,
which we offer you firstly
for your holy catholic Church.
Be pleased to grant her peace,
to guard, unite and govern her
throughout the whole world,
together with your servant N. our Pope
and N. our Bishop,
and all those who, holding to the truth,
hand on the catholic and apostolic faith.

Commemoration of the Living

Remember, Lord, your servants N. and N.
and all gathered here,
whose faith and devotion are known to you.
For them, we offer you this sacrifice of praise
or they offer it for themselves
and all who are dear to them:
for the redemption of their souls,
in hope of health and well-being,
and paying their homage to you,
the eternal God, living and true.

In communion with those whose memory we venerate,
especially the glorious ever-Virgin Mary,
Mother of our God and Lord, Jesus Christ,
*and blessed Joseph, her Spouse,
your blessed Apostles and Martyrs,
Peter and Paul, Andrew,
(James, John,
Thomas, James, Philip,
Bartholomew, Matthew,
Simon and Jude;
Linus, Cletus, Clement, Sixtus,
Cornelius, Cyprian,
Lawrence, Chrysogonus,
John and Paul,
Cosmas and Damian)
and all your Saints;
we ask that through their merits and prayers,
in all things we may be defended
by your protecting help.
(Through Christ our Lord. Amen.)

Hanc Igitur

Therefore, Lord, we pray:
graciously accept this oblation of our service,
the offering of your servants N. and N.
and of your whole family,
who entreat your majesty on their behalf;
and as you have brought them to their wedding day, so
(gladden them with your gift of
     the children they desire and)
bring them in your kindness
to the length of days for which they hope.
(Through Christ our Lord. Amen.)

---

* *On certain days this text has special insertions, which reflect the
     feast day.*

Be pleased, O God, we pray,
to bless, acknowledge,
and approve this offering in every respect;
make it spiritual and acceptable,
so that it may become for us
the Body and Blood of your most beloved Son,
our Lord Jesus Christ.

On the day before he was to suffer,
he took bread in his holy and venerable hands,
and with eyes raised to heaven
to you, O God, his almighty Father,
giving you thanks, he said the blessing,
broke the bread
and gave it to his disciples, saying:

TAKE THIS, ALL OF YOU, AND EAT OF IT,
FOR THIS IS MY BODY,
WHICH WILL BE GIVEN UP FOR YOU.

In a similar way, when supper was ended,
he took this precious chalice
in his holy and venerable hands,
and once more giving you thanks, he said the blessing
and gave the chalice to his disciples, saying:

TAKE THIS, ALL OF YOU, AND DRINK FROM IT,
FOR THIS IS THE CHALICE OF MY BLOOD,
THE BLOOD OF THE NEW AND ETERNAL COVENANT,
WHICH WILL BE POURED OUT FOR YOU AND FOR MANY
FOR THE FORGIVENESS OF SINS.

DO THIS IN MEMORY OF ME.

The mystery of faith.

**We proclaim your Death, O Lord,
and profess your Resurrection
until you come again.**

or

**When we eat this Bread and drink this Cup,
we proclaim your Death, O Lord,
until you come again.**

or

**Save us, Saviour of the world,
for by your Cross and Resurrection
you have set us free.**

Therefore, O Lord,
as we celebrate the memorial of the blessed Passion,
the Resurrection from the dead,
and the glorious Ascension into heaven
of Christ, your Son, our Lord,
we, your servants and your holy people,
offer to your glorious majesty
from the gifts that you have given us,
this pure victim,
this holy victim,
this spotless victim,
the holy Bread of eternal life
and the Chalice of everlasting salvation.

Be pleased to look upon these offerings
with a serene and kindly countenance,
and to accept them,
as once you were pleased to accept
the gifts of your servant Abel the just,
the sacrifice of Abraham, our father in faith,
and the offering of your high priest Melchizedek,
a holy sacrifice, a spotless victim.
In humble prayer we ask you, almighty God:

command that these gifts be borne
by the hands of your holy Angel
to your altar on high
in the sight of your divine majesty,
so that all of us,
    who through this participation at the altar
receive the most holy Body and Blood of your Son,
may be filled with every grace and heavenly blessing.
(Through Christ our Lord. Amen.)

Commemoration of the Dead

Remember also, Lord, your servants N. and N.,
who have gone before us with the sign of faith
and rest in the sleep of peace.
Grant them, O Lord, we pray,
and all who sleep in Christ,
a place of refreshment, light and peace.
(Through Christ our Lord. Amen.)

To us, also, your servants, who, though sinners,
hope in your abundant mercies,
graciously grant some share
and fellowship with your
    holy Apostles and Martyrs:
with John the Baptist, Stephen,
Matthias, Barnabas,
(Ignatius, Alexander,
Marcellinus, Peter,
Felicity, Perpetua,
Agatha, Lucy,
Agnes, Cecilia, Anastasia)
and all your Saints;
admit us, we beseech you,
into their company,
not weighing our merits,
but granting us your pardon,
through Christ our Lord.

Through whom
you continue to make all these good things,
    O Lord;
you sanctify them, fill them with life,
bless them, and bestow them upon us.

Through him, and with him, and in him,
O God, almighty Father,
in the unity of the Holy Spirit,
all glory and honour is yours,
for ever and ever.
Amen.

Then follows the Communion Rite, p. 21.

Eucharistic Prayer II

Priest: You are indeed Holy, O Lord,
the fount of all holiness.

Make holy, therefore, these gifts, we pray,
by sending down your Spirit upon them
    like the dewfall,
so that they may become for us
the Body and ✠ Blood of our Lord, Jesus Christ.

At the time he was betrayed
and entered willingly into his Passion,
he took bread and, giving thanks, broke it,
and gave it to his disciples, saying:

TAKE THIS, ALL OF YOU, AND EAT OF IT,
FOR THIS IS MY BODY,
WHICH WILL BE GIVEN UP FOR YOU.

In a similar way, when supper was ended,
he took the chalice
and, once more giving thanks,
he gave it to his disciples, saying:

TAKE THIS, ALL OF YOU, AND DRINK FROM IT,
FOR THIS IS THE CHALICE OF MY BLOOD,
THE BLOOD OF THE NEW AND ETERNAL COVENANT,
WHICH WILL BE POURED OUT FOR YOU AND FOR MANY
FOR THE FORGIVENESS OF SINS.

DO THIS IN MEMORY OF ME.

The mystery of faith.

**We proclaim your Death, O Lord,
and profess your Resurrection
until you come again.**

or

**When we eat this Bread and drink this Cup,
we proclaim your Death, O Lord,
until you come again.**

or

**Save us, Saviour of the world,
for by your Cross and Resurrection
you have set us free.**

Therefore, as we celebrate
the memorial of his Death and Resurrection,
we offer you, Lord,
the Bread of life and the Chalice of salvation,
giving thanks that you have held us worthy
to be in your presence and minister to you.

Humbly we pray
that, partaking of the Body and Blood of Christ,
we may be gathered into one by the Holy Spirit.

Remember, Lord, your Church,
spread throughout the world,
and bring her to the fullness of charity,
together with N. our Pope and N. our Bishop
and all the clergy.

Be mindful also, Lord, of N. and N.,
whom you have brought to their wedding day,
so that by your grace
they may abide in mutual love and in peace.

Remember also our brothers and sisters
who have fallen asleep in the hope of the resurrection,
and all who have died in your mercy:
welcome them into the light of your face.
Have mercy on us all, we pray,
that with the Blessed Virgin Mary, Mother of God,
with blessed Joseph, her Spouse,
with the blessed Apostles,
and all the Saints who have pleased you
    throughout the ages,
we may merit to be coheirs to eternal life,
and may praise and glorify you
through your Son, Jesus Christ.

Through him, and with him, and in him,
O God, almighty Father,
in the unity of the Holy Spirit,
all glory and honour is yours,
for ever and ever.
Amen.

Then follows the Communion Rite, p. 21.

Eucharistic Prayer III

Priest: You are indeed Holy, O Lord,
and all you have created
rightly gives you praise,
for through your Son our Lord Jesus Christ,
by the power and working of the Holy Spirit,
you give life to all things and make them holy,
and you never cease to gather a people to yourself,
so that from the rising of the sun to its setting
a pure sacrifice may be offered to your name.

Therefore, O Lord, we humbly implore you:
by the same Spirit graciously make holy
these gifts we have brought to you for consecration,
that they may become the Body and ✠ Blood
of your Son our Lord Jesus Christ,
at whose command we celebrate these mysteries.

For on the night he was betrayed
he himself took bread,
and, giving you thanks, he said the blessing,
broke the bread and gave it to his disciples, saying:

TAKE THIS, ALL OF YOU, AND EAT OF IT,
FOR THIS IS MY BODY,
WHICH WILL BE GIVEN UP FOR YOU.

In a similar way, when supper was ended,
he took the chalice,
and giving you thanks, he said the blessing,
and gave the chalice to his disciples, saying:

TAKE THIS, ALL OF YOU, AND DRINK FROM IT,
FOR THIS IS THE CHALICE OF MY BLOOD,
THE BLOOD OF THE NEW AND ETERNAL COVENANT,
WHICH WILL BE POURED OUT FOR YOU AND FOR MANY
FOR THE FORGIVENESS OF SINS.

DO THIS IN MEMORY OF ME.

The mystery of faith.

**We proclaim your Death, O Lord,
and profess your Resurrection
until you come again.**

or

**When we eat this Bread and drink this Cup,
we proclaim your Death, O Lord,
until you come again.**

or

**Save us, Saviour of the world,
for by your Cross and Resurrection
you have set us free.**

Therefore, O Lord, as we celebrate the memorial
of the saving Passion of your Son,
his wondrous Resurrection
and Ascension into heaven,
and as we look forward to his second coming,
we offer you in thanksgiving
this holy and living sacrifice.

Look, we pray, upon the oblation of your Church
and, recognising the sacrificial Victim by whose death
you willed to reconcile us to yourself,
grant that we, who are nourished
by the Body and Blood of your Son
and filled with his Holy Spirit,
may become one body, one spirit in Christ.

May he make of us
an eternal offering to you,
so that we may obtain an inheritance with your elect,
especially with the most Blessed Virgin Mary,
   Mother of God,

with blessed Joseph, her Spouse,
with your blessed Apostles and glorious Martyrs
(with Saint N.: the Saint of the day or Patron Saint)
and with all the Saints,
on whose constant intercession in your presence
we rely for unfailing help.

May this Sacrifice of our reconciliation,
we pray, O Lord,
advance the peace and salvation of all the world.
Be pleased to confirm in faith and charity
your pilgrim Church on earth,
with your servant N. our Pope and N. our Bishop,
the Order of Bishops, all the clergy,
and the entire people you have gained for your own.

Listen graciously to the prayers of this family,
whom you have summoned before you.
Strengthen, we pray, in the grace of Marriage
        N. and N.,
whom you have brought happily to their wedding day,
that under your protection
they may always be faithful in their lives
to the covenant they have sealed in your presence.
In your compassion, O merciful Father,
gather to yourself all your children
scattered throughout the world.

To our departed brothers and sisters
and to all who were pleasing to you
at their passing from this life,
give kind admittance to your kingdom.
There we hope to enjoy for ever
        the fullness of your glory
through Christ our Lord,
through whom you bestow on the world
        all that is good.

Through him, and with him, and in him,
O God, almighty Father,
in the unity of the Holy Spirit,
all glory and honour is yours,
for ever and ever.
Amen.

Then follows the Communion Rite, p. 21.

Appendix D

Nuptial Blessings

B

Let us pray to the Lord for this bride and groom,
who come to the altar as they begin their married life,
that (partaking of the Body and Blood of Christ)
they may always be bound together
    by love for one another.

All pray silently for a short while.

Holy Father,
who formed man in your own image,
male and female you created them,
so that as husband and wife, united in body and heart,
they might fulfil their calling in the world;

O God, who, to reveal the great design
    you formed in your love,
willed that the love of spouses for each other
should foreshadow the covenant
    you graciously made with your people,
so that, by fulfilment of the sacramental sign,
the mystical marriage of Christ with his Church
might become manifest
in the union of husband and wife among your faithful;

Graciously stretch out your right hand
over these your servants (N. and N.), we pray,
and pour into their hearts
    the power of the Holy Spirit.

Grant, O Lord,
that, as they enter upon this sacramental union,
they may share with one another the gifts of your love
and, by being for each other a sign of your presence,
become one heart and one mind.

May they also sustain, O Lord, by their deeds
the home they are forming
(and prepare their children
to become members of your heavenly household
by raising them in the way of the Gospel).

Graciously crown with your blessings
    your daughter N.,
so that, by being a good wife (and mother),
she may bring warmth to her home
    with a love that is pure
and adorn it with welcoming graciousness.

Bestow a heavenly blessing also, O Lord,
on N., your servant,
that he may be a worthy, good and
faithful husband (and a provident father).

Grant, holy Father,
that, desiring to approach your table
as a couple joined in Marriage in your presence,
they may one day have the joy
of taking part in your great banquet in heaven.
Through Christ our Lord.
Amen.

Then follows the Sign of Peace, p. 23.

C

Let us humbly invoke by our prayers,
    dear brothers and sisters,
God's blessing upon this bride and groom,
that in his kindness he may favour with his help
those on whom he has bestowed
    the Sacrament of Matrimony.

All pray silently for a short while.

Holy Father, maker of the whole world,
who created man and woman in your own image
and willed that their union be crowned
    with your blessing,
we humbly beseech you for these your servants,
who are joined today in the Sacrament of Matrimony.

May your abundant blessing, Lord,
come down upon this bride, N.,
and upon N., her companion for life,
and may the power of your Holy Spirit
set their hearts aflame from on high,
so that, living out together the gift of Matrimony,
they may (adorn their family with children
and) enrich the Church.

In happiness may they praise you, O Lord,
in sorrow may they seek you out;
may they have the joy of your presence
to assist them in their toil,
and know that you are near
to comfort them in their need;
let them pray to you in the holy assembly
and bear witness to you in the world,
and after a happy old age,
together with the circle of friends
    that surrounds them,
may they come to the Kingdom of Heaven.
Through Christ our Lord.
Amen.

Then follows the Sign of Peace, p. 23.

Appendix E

The Profession of Faith

The Niceno-Constantinopolitan Creed

I believe in one God,
the Father almighty,
maker of heaven and earth,
of all things visible and invisible.

I believe in one Lord Jesus Christ,
the Only Begotten Son of God,
born of the Father before all ages.
God from God, Light from Light,
true God from true God,
begotten, not made, consubstantial
   with the Father;
through him all things were made.
For us men and for our salvation
he came down from heaven,

(all bow during the next three lines)

and by the Holy Spirit was incarnate of the
   Virgin Mary,
and became man.

For our sake he was crucified under Pontius Pilate,
he suffered death and was buried,
and rose again on the third day
in accordance with the Scriptures.
He ascended into heaven
and is seated at the right hand of the Father.
He will come again in glory
to judge the living and the dead
and his kingdom will have no end.

I believe in the Holy Spirit, the Lord, the giver of life,
who proceeds from the Father and the Son,
who with the Father and the Son
   is adored and glorified,
who has spoken through the prophets.

I believe in one, holy, catholic and
    apostolic Church.
I confess one Baptism for the forgiveness
    of sins
and I look forward to the resurrection
    of the dead
and the life of the world to come. Amen.

or

The Apostles' Creed
I believe in God,
the Father almighty,
Creator of heaven and earth,
and in Jesus Christ, his only Son, our Lord,
(all bow during the next two lines)
who was conceived by the Holy Spirit,
born of the Virgin Mary,
suffered under Pontius Pilate,
was crucified, died and was buried;
he descended into hell;
on the third day he rose again from the dead;
he ascended into heaven,
and is seated at the right hand of God
    the Father almighty;
from there he will come to judge the living
    and the dead.

I believe in the Holy Spirit,
the holy catholic Church,
the communion of saints,
the forgiveness of sins,
the resurrection of the body,
and life everlasting. Amen.

Appendix F

The Prayer of the Faithful

(Bidding Prayers)

Any appropriate bidding prayers may be said. Some or all of those given here may be used, or others specially composed for the occasion.

Priest: Dear brothers and sisters,
as we call to mind the special gift of grace and charity
by which God has been pleased to crown and consecrate
the love of our sister N. and our brother N.,
let us commend them to the Lord.

Reader: That these faithful Christians, N. and N.,
newly joined in Holy Matrimony,
may always enjoy health and well-being,
let us pray to the Lord.
People: **Lord, we ask you, hear our prayer.**

That he will bless their covenant
as he chose to sanctify marriage at Cana in Galilee,
let us pray to the Lord.
Lord, we ask you, hear our prayer.

That they be granted perfect and fruitful love,
peace and strength,
and that they bear faithful witness
    to the name of Christian,
let us pray to the Lord.
Lord, we ask you, hear our prayer.

That the Christian people
may grow in virtue day by day
and that all who are burdened by any need
may receive the help of grace from above,
let us pray to the Lord.
Lord, we ask you, hear our prayer.

That the grace of the Sacrament
will be renewed by the Holy Spirit
in all married persons here present,
let us pray to the Lord.
Lord, we ask you, hear our prayer.

Let us pray for a while in silence.

Pause for silent prayer.

Priest: Graciously pour out
    upon this husband and wife, O Lord,
the Spirit of your love,
to make them one heart and one soul,
so that nothing whatever may divide
    those you have joined
and no harm come to those you have filled
    with your blessing.
Through Christ our Lord.
Amen.

The Mass continues on p. 17.

Hymns

1

Praise, my soul, the king of heaven;
to his feet thy tribute bring.
Ransomed, healed, restored, forgiven,
who like me his praise should sing?
Praise him! Praise him!
Praise him! Praise him!
Praise the everlasting king.

Praise him for his grace and favour
to our fathers in distress;
praise him still the same for ever,
slow to chide and swift to bless.
Praise him! Praise him!
Praise him! Praise him!
Glorious in his faithfulness.

Father-like, he tends and spares us;
well our feeble frame he knows;
in his hands he gently bears us,
rescues us from all our foes.
Praise him! Praise him!
Praise him! Praise him!
Widely as his mercy flows.

Angels, help us to adore him;
ye behold him face to face;
sun and moon, bow down before him;
dwellers all in time and space.
Praise him! Praise him!
Praise him! Praise him!
Praise with us the God of grace.

Henry F. Lyte (1793-1847)

2

Come down, O love divine,
seek thou this soul of mine,
and visit it with thine own ardour glowing;
O Comforter, draw near,
within my heart appear,
and kindle it, thy holy flame bestowing.

O let it freely burn,
till earthly passions turn
to dust and ashes in its heat consuming;
and let thy glorious light
shine ever on my sight,
and clothe me round, the while my path illuming.

Let holy charity
mine outward vesture be,
and lowliness become mine inner clothing;
true lowliness of heart,
which takes the humbler part,
and o'er its own shortcomings weeps with loathing.

And so the yearning strong,
with which the soul will long,
shall far outpass the power of human telling,
for none can guess its grace,
till he become the place
wherein the Holy Spirit makes a dwelling.

Bianco of Siena (d.1434)

3

Lead us, heavenly Father, lead us
o'er the world's tempestuous sea;
guard us, guide us, keep us, feed us,
for we have no help but thee;
yet possessing ev'ry blessing
if our God our Father be.

Saviour, breathe forgiveness o'er us,
all our weakness thou dost know;
thou didst tread this earth before us,
thou didst feel its keenest woe;
lone and dreary, faint and weary,
through the desert thou didst go.

Spirit of our God, descending,
fill our hearts with heavenly joy,
love with every passion blending,
pleasure that can never cloy:
thus provided, pardoned, guided,
nothing can our peace destroy.

James Edmeston (1791-1867)

4

Amazing grace! How sweet the sound
that saved a wretch like me.
I once was lost but now I'm found,
was blind, but now I see.

'Twas grace that taught my heart to fear,
and grace my fears relieved.
How precious did that grace appear
the hour I first believed.

Through many dangers, toils and snares
I have already come.
'Tis grace hath brought me safe thus far,
and grace will lead me home.

The Lord has promised good to me;
his word my hope secures.
He will my shield and portion be
as long as life endures.

John Newton (1725-1807)

5

O bread of heaven, beneath this veil
thou dost my very God conceal:
my Jesus, dearest treasure, hail;
I love thee and adoring kneel;
each loving soul by thee is fed
with thy own self in form of bread.

O food of life, thou who dost give
the pledge of immortality;
I live; no, 'tis not I that live;
God gives me life, God lives in me:
he feeds my soul, he guides my ways,
and every grief with joy repays.

O bond of love, that dost unite
the servant to his living Lord;
could I dare live and not requite
such love – then death were meet reward:
I cannot live unless to prove
some love for such unmeasured love.

Beloved Lord in heaven above,
there, Jesus, thou awaitest me;
to gaze on thee with changeless love;
yes, thus I hope, thus shall it be:
for how can he deny me heaven
who here on earth himself hath given?

St Alphonsus Liguori (1696-1787)

6

Dear Lord and Father of mankind,
forgive our foolish ways!
Re-clothe us in our rightful mind,
in purer lives thy service find,
in deeper reverence praise.

In simple trust like theirs who heard,
beside the Syrian sea,
the gracious calling of the Lord,
let us, like them, without a word,
rise up and follow thee.

O Sabbath rest by Galilee!
O calm of hills above,
where Jesus knelt to share with thee
the silence of eternity,
interpreted by love!

Drop thy still dews of quietness
till all our strivings cease;
take from our souls the strain and stress,
and let our ordered lives confess
the beauty of thy peace.

Breathe through the heats of our desire
thy coolness and thy balm;
let sense be dumb, let flesh retire;
speak through the earthquake, wind and fire,
O still small voice of calm!

John G. Whittier (1807-1892)

Love divine, all loves excelling,
joy of heaven, to earth come down,
fix in us thy humble dwelling,
all thy faithful mercies crown.

Jesus, thou art all compassion,
pure unbounded love thou art;
visit us with thy salvation,
enter every trembling heart.

Come, almighty to deliver,
let us all thy life receive;
suddenly return, and never,
never more thy temples leave.

Thee we would be always blessing,
serve thee as thy hosts above;
pray, and praise thee without ceasing,
glory in thy perfect love.

Finish then thy new creation,
pure and sinless let us be;
let us see thy great salvation,
perfectly restored in thee.

Changed from glory into glory,
till in heaven we take our place,
till we cast our crowns before thee,
lost in wonder, love and praise.

Charles Wesley (1707-1788)

Guide me, O thou great Redeemer,
pilgrim through this barren land;
I am weak, but thou art mighty,
hold me with thy pow'rful hand:
bread of heaven,
feed me till I want no more.

Open now the crystal fountain,
whence the healing stream doth flow;
let the fire and cloudy pillar
lead me all my journey through;
strong Deliverer,
be thou still my strength and shield.

When I tread the verge of Jordan,
bid my anxious fears subside;
death of death, and hell's destruction,
land me safe on Canaan's side;
songs of praises
I will ever give to thee.

William Williams (1717-1791)

9

Now thank we all our God,
with heart and hands and voices,
who wondrous things hath done,
in whom his world rejoices;
who from our mother's arms
hath blessed us on our way
with countless gifts of love,
and still is ours today.

O may this bounteous God
through all our life be near us,
with ever joyful hearts
and blessed peace to cheer us;
and keep us in his grace,
and guide us when perplexed,
and free us from all ills
in this world and the next.

All praise and thanks to God
the Father now be given,
the Son, and him who reigns
with them in highest heaven,
the one eternal God,
whom earth and heaven adore,
for thus it was, is now,
and shall be evermore.

Martin Rinkart (1586-1649)

The Lord's my shepherd, I'll not want;
he makes me down to lie
in pastures green: he leadeth me
the quiet waters by.

My soul he doth restore again;
and me to walk doth make
within the paths of righteousness
ev'n for his own name's sake.

Yea, though I walk in death's dark vale,
yet will I fear none ill:
for thou art with me; and thy rod
and staff me comfort still.

My table thou hast furnishèd
in presence of my foes.
My head thou dost with oil anoint
and my cup overflows.

Goodness and mercy all my life
shall surely follow me:
and in God's house for evermore
my dwelling-place shall be.

Scottish Psalter, 1650